I0016265

UI DESIGN
SKETCH BOOK

Dotted grid sheets for sketching out wireframes and drawing UI components

In case of loss, please return to:

_____

_____

_____

_____

_____

Create Compositions Easily

Use this book to create your layout sketches and compositions in a flexible and brilliantly simple tool that is ideal for daily use. Infuse this book with your projects, passions, imagination, culture, memories, and personal identity. Enjoy!

This sketchbook is part of a family of teaching and learning materials: sketchbooks, bullet journals, flash cards, and other tools for reading/writing/presenting design projects for modern people on the go.

You can find these books available at **www.amazon.com**.

I'd love to hear about your experience with any of the books or resources.

@soujohn   @soujohn1

How to Use This Book

The grid on these pages are based on a 8-point grid system. This grid helps define a base unit of measurement to help ensure pixel perfect details for all the elements in your wireframes (margin, spacing, font size, leading, alignment, etc). You can use the grid to create close-ups of individual components and/or an overview page with all the components placed within it.

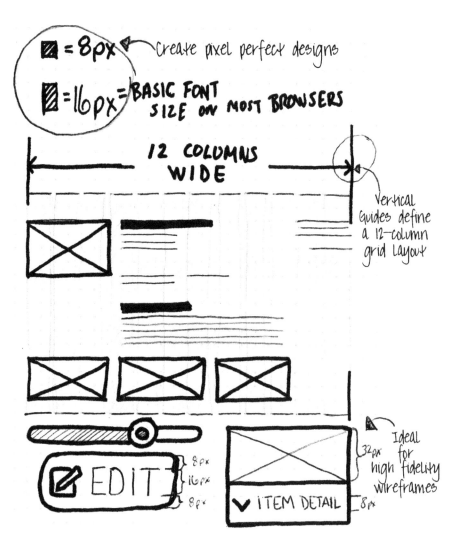

As you create your sketches consider using icons wherever they can help emphasize the detail or action you're planning for. The list of icons below can be used to indicate different UI elements.

Menu - displays grouped navigation actions

Settings - modify system options

Cart, Basket, Bag

Share

Account, Profile - edit/modify user preferences

Edit - make changes or changes are possible

Slider - allow the user to manually adjust a value in small increments

Search - allows the user to query for results based on search terms provided

Comment - user feedback

Carousel - allows users to browse through a set of items (images) that are usually hyperlinked

Payment, E-Commerce

Info, Notification, Alert, Pop-up, Warning

Upload / Download

Like, Favorite, Save / Rating System

List View / Grid View - toggle or switch display settings

Cancel - place this around an item to depict its opposite

Delete, Remove

Options - checkboxes (multiple choice) radio Buttons (single choice)

Location - find location, current location, mark location

2-State Settings - on/off, activate, deactivate

THANK YOU

Thank you for purchasing and making use of this design resource.

If you have comments and would like to share your thoughts on the <u>UI Design Sketchbook</u>, please reach out on social media.

Also, if you got a hold of this book at no cost consider making an investment in good karma by telling other people about it.

I'd love to hear about your experience with any of the books or resources.

@soujohn   @soujohn1

MORE RESOURCES

Square Grid Notebook

6"x9" portrait format

Square grid sheets for note-taking, sketching, wireframing, and doodling out drawings.

Daily Bullet Journal

6"x9" portrait format

A structured bullet journal with tick mark guides for creating sketches, notes, and wireframes.

Lettering Grid Notebook

8"x6" landscape format

Lettering grid sheets for planning and composing basic letters, strokes, and other details.

Hex Grid Notebook

8"x6" landscape format

Hex grid sheets for sketching and planning out maps, ideas, and details.

If you enjoyed this book, you can find more resources available at
www.amazon.com.

www.ingramcontent.com/pod-product-compliance
Lightning Source LLC
Chambersburg PA
CBHW070836070326
40690CB00009B/1570